A Family in Bolivia

A pronunciation guide for the Spanish and Indian names and words used in this book appears on page 28.

Map on pages 4-5 by James Michael Roy. Photographs on pages 22 and 23 (top) by Ed Fuentes.

LIBRARY OF CONGRESS CATALOGING-IN-PUBLICATION DATA

St. John, Jetty.
    A family in Bolivia.

    Summary: Describes the home, school, work, customs, amusements, and day-to-day activities of a young Bolivian boy and his family—living on the island of Suriqui in Lake Titicaca.
    1. Bolivia—Social life and customs—Juvenile literature.
2. Children—Bolivia—Juvenile literature. 3. Family—Bolivia—Juvenile literature. [1. Bolivia—Social life and customs.
2. Family life—Bolivia] I. Araneda, José Armando, ill. II. Title.
F3310.S73   1987   984   86-21034
ISBN 0-8225-1670-5 (lib. bdg.)

Manufactured in the United States of America

1 2 3 4 5 6 7 8 9 10 95 94 93 92 91 90 89 88 87

A Family in Bolivia

Jetty St. John

Photographs by José Armando Araneda

L Lerner Publications Company · Minneapolis

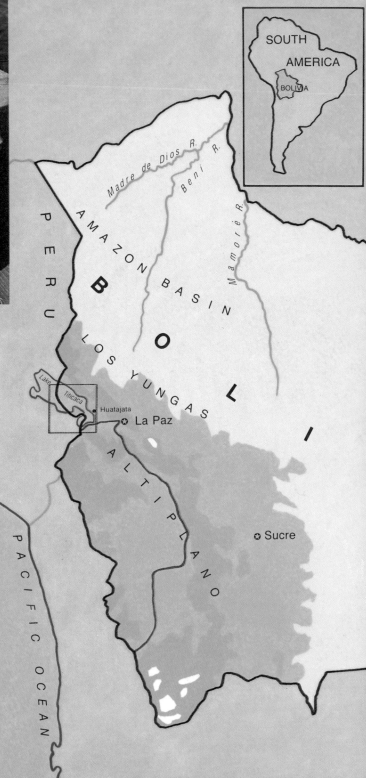

Porfirio is eleven years old. He lives in Bolivia on the island of Suriqui. His house looks out onto Lake Titicaca, which is the highest lake in the world. To the east and west he can see the rugged, snow-covered peaks of the Andes. The highest mountain is over 20,000 feet (6,000 meters) high.

The people around the lake are Indians whose ancestors lived there over 3,000 years ago. They speak an ancient language called Aymara. Bolivia was invaded 2,000 years ago by Incas from Peru. The Incan language, Quechua, is still widely spoken.

4

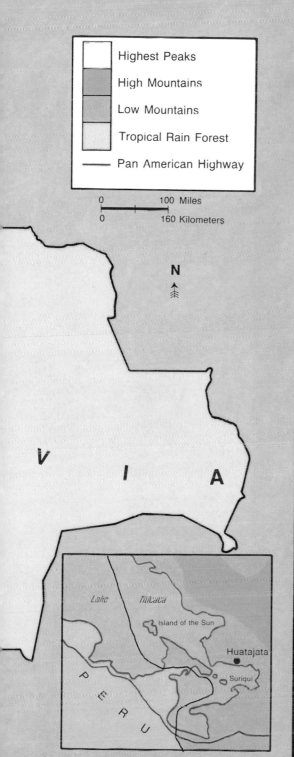

Highest Peaks
High Mountains
Low Mountains
Tropical Rain Forest
— Pan American Highway

0   100 Miles
0   160 Kilometers

N

Lake Titicaca
Island of the Sun
Huatajata
Suriqui
PERU

Five hundred years ago, Spanish conquerors came to Bolivia in search of gold. They defeated the Incas and built their own cities. Today, people in the cities speak Spanish.

To the south of Lake Titicaca there is a barren plateau, the Altiplano. It stretches for almost 800 miles. Most Bolivians live in cities on the northern end of the plateau. The southern part is desert. A few mining towns in the south supply minerals such as tin, silver, and copper.

East of the mountains, the land slopes away toward the Amazon basin where there are dense tropical forests. On the slopes are fertile valleys, called the Yungas, where all kinds of potatoes and fruits are grown.

Porfirio's father, Señor Esteban, is a boat builder. He makes wooden sailing craft and *balsas de totora*, or boats of reed.

Each morning Porfirio's mother, Señora Esteban, collects reeds near the shore of the lake. Some of the reeds are dried and are burned to provide heat for cooking. Wet reeds are given to the *llamas* to eat.

Before school, Rosita, who is 13, drives the sheep from the back yard and turns them loose to graze all day on the hillside behind the house. The Estebans raise sheep mainly for their wool. They eat lamb or mutton only at festival time or on special occasions.

Cousin Freddy stops by for Porfirio so they can walk to school together. The *lluchus*, or woolen hats, are comfortable and offer protection from the wind and bright sun. Señora Esteban knitted them.

Children can go to school from age seven to age fourteen. School begins at 9:00 A.M. and lasts until 4:00 P.M. Everyone goes home for one hour at lunch. Freddy usually eats with Porfirio.

The winter vacation is in June and July. Then the weather is dry and sunny, but at night it gets cold. Temperatures often fall below zero.

The summer vacation is from October to December. In the summer it is warm and wet. Porfirio likes winter best, when the days are clear and he can play outside.

Classes on Suriqui are taught in Aymara, but Porfirio is also learning Spanish. He knows some Spanish words already because they are also used in Aymara. *Sombrero de cholita*, for example, means the bowler hat worn by a girl or a woman.

After school the children often come to visit Señor Esteban. They enjoy looking in his museum and hearing his stories. He was one of the four Indians from Lake Titicaca who built large, ocean-going reed boats. One, called *Ra II*, sailed across the Pacific. Another, *Tigris*, sailed down the Persian Gulf. Señor Esteban tells about his travels, and the children look at model boats. Porfirio is learning to make the boats too.

A balsa de totora is made from reeds which are cut and then dried in the sun. The reeds are sorted and strapped into tight bundles to form the base, the sides, and the *yampu*, or heart of the boat.

The sections are bound together with a braided reed rope, which is over thirty feet long. The boat weighs about 45 pounds (100 kilograms) when it is finished. The sail is also made from reeds.

A well-made boat will last for a year and can be used for fishing on the lake. Porfirio's family keeps their balsa near the house so it dries out after each use on the lake. They have to watch the llama or he will eat it.

In the morning, everyone in the family drinks a cup of *mate de coca* for breakfast. This tea is often drunk with sugar and is good for *soroche*, or altitude sickness. Visitors often get soroche if they are not used to breathing the thin mountain air.

Most evenings, the family eats soup made with wheat flour or noodles. This is eaten with potatoes and *ocas*, another kind of root vegetable. There are over two hundred kinds of potatoes grown in Bolivia.

For lunch, Señora Esteban prepares fresh fish from the lake. Porfirio's older brother, Fermin, goes out early in the morning and nets the fish from a wooden sailboat. Señora Esteban serves the fish with potatoes. The Estebans eat potatoes, rice, or noodles at almost every meal.

Fermin's wife, Candelaria, helps Señora Esteban cook. The Estebans eat breakfast and lunch outside unless it's raining. It's dark by the time they eat their evening meal, so they usually have it inside the house.

After lunch, Candelaria works on a camera strap. She will sell the strap when she finishes weaving it.

Señora Esteban weaves a blanket. The wool comes from their llamas, which are shorn every two or three years.

In Bolivia, llamas are used as pack animals. They can carry heavy loads all day on rough tracks. Their thick coats also protect them from the cold.

Sometimes Porfirio, Fermin, and their father sail to the Island of the Sun to visit their friend, Señor Tipaña. He has an *alpaca*. This animal is like a llama, but has a softer coat and is not used to carry heavy loads.

The wool from the llama or alpaca is spun into yarn on an *huso* or spool. Often it is dipped into a vegetable dye to change its color.

The island is a place where the Incas once worshipped the sun. According to the legend, the sun rose out of Lake Titicaca and from that sun the great Inca leader Viracocha was born. This event is marked by a sacred rock on the northwest end of the island which people still visit.

There are ruins on the island, and steep stone Inca steps lead up the hill to Señor Tipaña's house. Next to the house there is a small Roman Catholic Church.

Many of the islanders play musical instruments such as the *zampoña*, or the *quena*, which is a kind of flute. People often get together for dances to celebrate festivals and national holidays.

Señor Tipaña plays his zampoña for his guests. He made it himself out of bamboo that came from the Yungas.

At home on Suriqui, Fermin practices his accordian while his friends play the guitar and banjo. Sometimes they go to La Paz to sing, and there they made a record of folk dances.

La Paz is used as Bolivia's capital. It is the highest capital city in the world. Over 400 years ago, Spaniards built this city because they found gold in the river there. They built it in a basin which protects it from the cold winds that blow across the Altiplano.

Small houses are tucked high on the hillside. Lower down are the skyscrapers and offices of the business district.

At the base of the valley there are larger homes and a sports stadium. The stadium was built at a lower altitude so athletes would not suffer soroche when they play there. Soccer games are played at the stadium.

Many people bring fruit and vegetables to La Paz to sell on the streets and open-air markets. Some barbeque meat, and others sell mate de coca, or fresh juice squeezed from fruits such as papayas or mangos grown in the tropical regions.

Señor Esteban and Fermin work with other boat builders on Suriqui to build wooden sailboats which are used for fishing and for transport across the lake. The sound of hammers can be heard all over the village.

They use cedar wood, which comes from the slopes of the Yungas. Supplies such as nails and sailcloth are bought in La Paz.

To get supplies, Señor Esteban travels first by boat to the mainland, and then by bus to the city. The bus ride takes about two hours, and there are frequent stops. Many people climb on with their produce or crafts which they sell in the markets.

Fermin sometimes takes his mother, his wife, and his sister Rosita by boat to watch celebrations on the mainland. Depending on the wind, it can take a day to sail to Huatajata, the nearest village.

For festivals, the women dress up in bright clothes and the men play musical instruments. For the harvest festival, the women carry bright flowers. The dancers move along the shore of the lake. They go towards the village square, then they dance late into the night. Some celebrations last for a number of days.

Porfirio stays at home with his father. He works on his model boat. His father watches to see that each section of the balsa is even and tight. One day Porfirio hopes he will build as well as his father.

Spanish and Indian Words in This Book

Although Porfirio and his family speak Aymara, they also use some Spanish and some Quechuan words and phrases. The letter in front of each word or phrase below tells which language it is from. "S" stands for Spanish, "A" for Aymara, and "Q" for Quechua. Where there is more than one letter, the phrase is made up of words from more than one language.

A	**alpaca** al-PACK-ah		A	**oca** OAH-kah
S	**Altiplano** al-tee-PLAH-noh		A	**Porfirio** pour-FEE-ree-oh
A	**Aymara** eye-MAR-uh		Q	**Quechua** ket-CHOO-ah
S, A	**balsa de totora** BALL-zoh day tot-ORE-ah		Q	**quena** KAN-ah
S	**Bolivia** boh-LIV-ee-uh		S	**Rosita** rose-EE-tah
S	**Candelaria** can-deh-LAH-ree-ah		S, A	**sombrero de cholita** zomb-BRAIR-row day cho-LEE-tah
S	**Esteban** es-TAY-ban		Q	**soroche** sore-OH-che
S	**Fermin** FAIR-meen		A	**Suriqui** soor-EE-kee
A	**Huatajata** what-ah-HA-tah		A	**Tipaña** tee-PAN-yah
A	**huso** OO-zoh		Q	**Titicaca** tit-ee-KAH-KAH
A	**llama** YAH-mah		Q	**Viracocha** veer-ah-COACH-ah
A	**lluchu** LOOT-chew		A	**yampu** YAM-poh
A	**mate de coca** ma-TAY day COH-kah		A	**Yungas** YOONG-gahs
			A	**zampoña** zom-PONE-yah

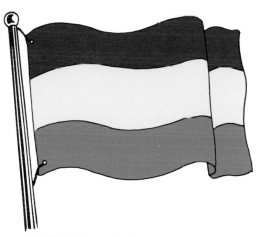

This the national flag of Bolivia, flown by the people of the country. The government uses the state flag, which includes the state seal (a drawing of crossed flags, a condor, an alpaca, a mountain, a breadfruit tree and wheat sheaf) in the yellow stripe.

Facts about Bolivia

Capital: Sucre (official)
La Paz (actual)

Languages: Spanish, Quechua, Aymara

Form of Money: Bolivian peso

Area: 424,164 square miles (1,098,581 square kilometers)

Population: About 6.25 million people
Bolivia has just under half as many people as Texas, and is almost twice as large. Almost three-fourths of the people are Aymara or Quechuan.

NORTH
AMERICA

SOUTH
AMERICA

Bolivia

EUROPE

ASIA

AFRICA

AUSTRALIA

31

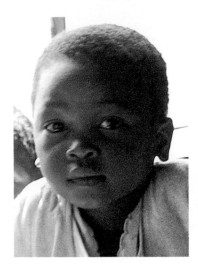

Families the World Over

Some children in foreign countries live like you do. Others live very differently. In these books, you can meet children from all over the world. You'll learn about their games and schools, their families and friends, and what it's like to grow up in a faraway land.

AN ABORIGINAL FAMILY	AN ESKIMO FAMILY	A FAMILY IN MOROCCO
AN ARAB FAMILY	A FAMILY IN FRANCE	A FAMILY IN NIGERIA
A FAMILY IN AUSTRALIA	A FAMILY IN INDIA	A FAMILY IN PAKISTAN
A FAMILY IN BOLIVIA	A FAMILY IN IRELAND	A FAMILY IN PERU
A FAMILY IN BRAZIL	A FAMILY IN ITALY	A FAMILY IN SINGAPORE
A FAMILY IN CHILE	A FAMILY IN JAMAICA	A FAMILY IN SRI LANKA
A FAMILY IN CHINA	A FAMILY IN JAPAN	A FAMILY IN WEST GERMANY
A FAMILY IN EGYPT	A FAMILY IN LIBERIA	A ZULU FAMILY

Lerner Publications Company
241 First Avenue North
Minneapolis, Minnesota 55401